THE BATTLE OF THE LITTLE BIGHORN

THE BATTLE OF THE LITTLE BIGHORN

Charles A. Wills

Silver Burdett Press, Inc.
Englewood Cliffs, New Jersey

Acknowledgments

The author thanks the following individuals and institutions for their invaluable help in text and picture research: Ms. Kelly Blythin, the Library of Congress; Mr. Douglas C. McChristian, Chief Historian, Custer Battlefield National Monument; Ms. Pat Stein of the American Archives, Inc.; and the South Dakota Division of Tourism.

Consultants

We thank the following people for reviewing the manuscript and offering their helpful suggestions:

Arnold Markoe
Professor
Brooklyn College
The City University of New York

Robert M. Goldberg
Department Chairman, Social Studies
Team Leader of Interdisciplinary Group of Academic Teachers
Oceanside Middle School
Oceanside, New York

Cover: This painting by J.K. Ralston, The Last Bugle, captures of the fury of the Bighorn fight. Courtesy of the Custer Battlefield National Monument.

Title Page: Red Horse, a Sioux council chief, painted this version of the battle in 1881. Courtesy of the Smithsonian Institution.

Contents Page: This Winchester rifle, its stock decorated with tacks, belonged to Sitting Bull. Courtesy of the Smithsonian Institution.

Back Cover: Detail of Red Horse's painting of the Battle of the Little Bighorn. Courtesy of the Smithsonian Institution.

Library of Congress Catagloging-in-Publication Data

Wills, Charles.
   The battle of the Little Bighorn/Charles A. Wills.
     p. cm. —(Turning points in American History.)
   Summary: Describes the warfare between whites and Great Plains Indians in the nineteenth century, with an emphasis on the famous massacre at Little Bighorn.
   Includes bibliographical references.
   1. Little Big Horn, Battle of the, 1876—Juvenile literature. [1. Little Big Horn, Battle of the, 1876. 2. Indians of North America—Great Plains—Wars.] I. Title. II. Series: Turning points in American history.
E83.876.W49   1990
973.8'2—dc20
                        90-8419
                        CIP
                        AC

Editorial Coordination by Richard G. Gallin

 Created by Media Projects Incorporated

C. Carter Smith, *Executive Editor*
Toni Rachiele, *Managing Editor*
Charles A. Wills, *Project Editor*
Bernard Schleifer, *Design Consultant*
Arlene Goldberg, *Cartographer*

Manufactured in the United States of America.

ISBN 0-382-09952-4 [lib. bdg.]
10 9 8 7 6 5 4 3 2 1

ISBN 0-382-09948-6 [pbk.]
10 9 8 7 6 5 4 3 2 1

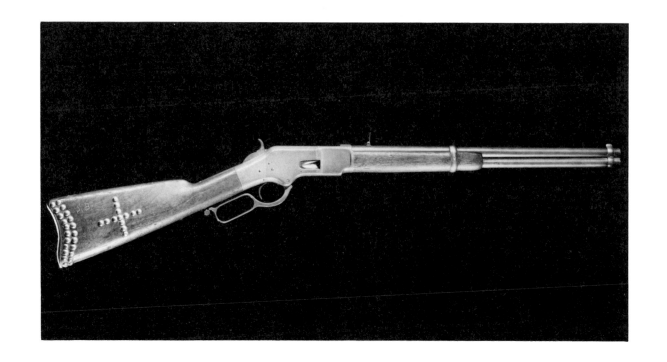

CONTENTS

INTRODUCTION

"WHERE IS CUSTER?"

General Alfred Terry, U.S. Army, adjusted his broad-brimmed hat against the blazing Montana sunshine. It was Monday morning, June 26, 1876.

Terry sat astride his horse, his eyes scanning the sun-scorched plains. He was quiet. However, the officers and men around him were chattering excitedly.

A few moments before, Lieutenant James Bradley had arrived in camp with his detachment of Crow Indian scouts. They told a terrible story. They had met three other Indian scouts a few miles ahead, along the Bighorn River. The scouts were from Lieutenant Colonel George Custer's Seventh Cavalry Regiment. They said Custer and all his men had ridden into a great Indian encampment in the valley of the Little Bighorn River. Neither he nor any of his men had come out alive.

The hill of the last stand as it looks today.

Terry's troopers scoffed at the scouts' story. The Seventh was an elite unit, organized to pursue Plains Indians who chose to ignore the commands of the "Great Father" in Washington. Custer himself had been in the West for a decade, on and off, and he was veteran of many hard-fought campaigns. Such a man, Terry's troopers insisted, could not have met defeat and death at the hands of a ragged band of Sioux and Cheyenne, here in the wilderness of the Montana Territory. Besides, they had seen smoke rising from the plains ahead. That could mean only one thing: Custer had defeated the Sioux and their Cheyenne allies, and now he was burning their camp.

General Terry did not share his troops' disbelief. He knew Custer was brave. He also knew Custer could be reckless. He remembered his last talk with Custer, as he and his men left to search for the braves of Sitting Bull and Crazy Horse. Instead of issuing specific orders, Terry had given Custer freedom

White-Man-Runs-Him, one of Custer's Crow Indian scouts. The crows were a traditional enemy of the Sioux and helped the army in its campaigns.

to do as he liked: "Use your own judgment, and do what you think is best if you strike the trail; and whatever you do, Custer, hold on to your wounded." Now he regretted his words.

General Terry wanted to find out the truth. "I'll give two hundred dollars to any man who breaks through to Custer," he said. Soon afterward, Lieutenant Charles Roe left camp with a troop of cavalry. Soon they sighted some horsemen clad in the blue uniform of the U.S. Army. One man held Custer's personal flag: crossed swords on a blue and red background. They must be Custer's men, thought Roe. He and his horseman rode out to meet them. Suddenly bullets zinged overhead. Lieutenant Roe realized, with a shock, that they were Sioux dressed in army uniforms. Roe and his troopers retreated in a hurry.

That night, Terry's men were nervous as they munched hardtack and bacon around their campfires. They knew that they would be moving forward in the morning. Whatever they encountered would solve the mystery of what had happened to Custer.

Tuesday, June 27, was as hot as Monday had been. As the cavalrymen rode, they peered through the heat haze and saw strange white shapes in the valley ahead. No one could figure out what they were.

They came on an abandoned Indian camp. A trooper dismounted and held his hand over the ashes of a campfire; they were still warm. Other men discovered a variety of debris—letters and pictures, tin cups, saddles. A surgeon found a pair of gloves marked "Yates, 7th Cav." Another man saw a shirt that he knew belonged to one of Custer's officers. It was caked with blood.

Something terrible *had* happened to Custer and his men. Terry's men reached the white shapes. They were the bodies of Seventh Cavalry soldiers. Most were stripped and terribly mutilated. Custer's body was found. Strangely, it hadn't been touched.

A few hours later Terry's men saw other soldiers ahead, cheering their approach. These were troopers of Major

Marcus Reno and Captain Fred Benteen. They had been trapped by the Sioux and Cheyenne on a small hill for almost two days and had suffered heavy casualties. Then, suddenly, the Indians had broken camp and left.

Throughout their ordeal, the troopers had wondered why Custer had not returned to help them.

"Where is Custer?" asked Captain Benteen anxiously.

"To the best of my knowledge," Terry replied, "he lies on this ridge about four miles below here with all his command killed."

Benteen did not believe Terry at first. The general told him to see for himself. Benteen walked down into the valley of the Little Bighorn River. He was pale and shaken when he returned.

The soldiers fashioned stretchers for the wounded and started moving to the Yellowstone River, where the steamship *Far West* waited.

The *Far West* reached Fort Lincoln, the expedition's headquarters, a week later. Custer's personal band stood on the riverbank with their instruments in their hands, about to begin a concert in honor of the United States's centennial. It was July 4, 1876, the one-hundredth anniversary of the country's independence. The conductor raised his hands, about to begin a patriotic song, when the *Far West*'s whistle split the air.

Soon, the telegraph, which the Indians called the "talking wire," began tap-

General George A. Custer.

ping out the story of Custer's defeat to a shocked nation.

Somehow, many Indians already knew what had happened at the Little Bighorn. A few days before, a Paiute Indian in Indian Territory (now the state of Oklahoma) had told a white man that Custer and all his men had died at the hands of the Sioux. The white man had laughed at this ridiculous tale.

The Indian Territory was more than a thousand miles south of the Little Bighorn. How had the Indians known of Custer's defeat before the rest of the country? Messengers? Smoke signals? To this day, no one knows.

1

THE PEOPLE OF DREAMS

The Great Plains of North America lie between the hundredth parallel of longitude and the Rocky Mountains. This vast region stretches from Canada to the Texas panhandle, covering much of what is now the states of North and South Dakota, Nebraska, Kansas, Oklahoma, Montana, Texas, Colorado, and Wyoming.

For centuries the Plains were grassland. Even today there are few trees in the region. Rivers twist through the land, but little rain falls. On the Plains, summers can be blazing hot and winters are usually bitterly cold. Tornadoes, blizzards, and other storms often sweep across the land.

When white people came to the Plains they found it a harsh land. They were used to the hills and forests of Europe and the eastern parts of North America. Also, they believed crops

A Plains Indian warrior, as painted by George Catlin.

wouldn't grow on land without trees. Explorers like Zebulon Pike and Stephen Long, who crossed the Great Plains early in the nineteenth century, called it "The Great American Desert." The grassy, windswept Plains, Long said, were "wholly unfit for cultivation" by farmers. There was scarcely enough wood and water to support travelers, let alone settlers.

But to the people who had roamed the Plains for centuries, the Native Americans (American Indians), the land was anything but a desert. The Plains provided them with everything they needed to survive, and they created a remarkable culture.

There were many different groups of Indians on the Plains: the Blackfoot, Crow, and Sioux to the north; Arapaho, Shoshone, and Pawnee in the central Plains; and Kiowa and Comanche in the South. Within these groups there were many smaller groups. The Sioux, for example, were split into eastern and western groups, and within those groups there were many tribal bands—Miniconjou, Brule, Hunkpapa, and others.

Although there were many differences among the Plains Indian groups, including language, they shared a common culture and all could understand sign language. They had no feeling of themselves as "Indians"; rather, each group of tribes considered itself unique. The names of most tribes, when translated into English, mean "the people" or "the nation."

Relationships among the groups ranged from friendship to bitter hostility. One group might have friendly relations with one neighbor, but consider another group to be deadly enemies. The Sioux, for example, hunted and traded with the Cheyenne, their neighbors to the south, but they were enemies of the Crow to their west.

Two animals, the buffalo and the horse, influenced the life and culture of the Plains Indians more than anything else. The buffalo, also called the bison, is a shaggy animal that can weigh as much as a ton. Before the mid-nineteenth century, vast herds of buffalo grazed on the Plains. As many as 50 million may have roamed the Plains

A buffalo bull.

only two centuries ago. The Sioux called the slow-moving animals *pte*—wise uncle. The buffalo provided the Indian with many things. Its meat was a staple of the diet. In the summer, the hunting season, it was eaten fresh and preserved for the winter. From buffalo hide came clothing and material for the *tipi*, the conical tent that most Plains Indians lived in. The buffalo's sinews (tendons) were twisted into cord and bowstrings, its bones were carved into tools, and its horns were made into eating utensils. The animal's dung was used for fuel on the treeless Plains.

The buffalo was a migratory animal—it moved from place to place with the seasons. For that reason, the Plains Indians were nomadic—a people who moved frequently rather than settling permanently in one spot. For much of their early history, Plains tribes practiced farming on a small scale and followed the buffalo in the summertime. Their main beast of burden was the dog. Crossed sticks were lashed to the dog's back to form a platform, now called a *travois*, to carry possessions. Before the eighteenth century, the Indians hunted the buffalo on foot, which was a dangerous business. A trapped herd might stampede a hunting party, and a wounded buffalo could crush a hunter beneath its great bulk.

Around the middle of the eighteenth century, the Plains Indians started to use horses, and within a century, the horse transformed the Plains Indian's society.

Horses are not native to the Plains.

They were brought there by Spanish colonists in what is now the Southwest of the United States. These Spanish horses were small and swift. They could survive the bitter winters by foraging for grass in the snow. Over time, horses escaped from these settlements, until eventually great herds of wild horses roamed the Plains. The first Indians to encounter wild horses did not know what to do with them. Often they were hunted and eaten. But the tribes of the Southwest and the southern Plains learned in time to domesticate the horse. The northern tribes quickly followed their example.

By the nineteenth century, the Plains Indians were among the finest horsemen on earth. George Catlin, a white explorer and artist, wrote of the Comanche in 1834: "A Comanche on the ground is awkward . . . but the moment he lays his hand upon his horse, his face becomes even handsome, and he gracefully flies away like a different being."

The horse radically changed the way the Indians lived. They could now travel faster and farther in their pursuit of the buffalo, and hunting was easier and safer from horseback. With their source of food secure, the people of the Plains prospered. They could devote time to their religion, to crafts, and to war.

War was an important part of the Plains Indian's life. Fighting was constant and often cruel. The Indians did not care for prisoners—a captured warrior could expect to be tortured and killed. But war, for the Plains tribes, had a special purpose.

Plains Indians on horseback hunt buffalo.

Tribes might fight each other for horses or to drive their enemy from favored hunting grounds. But war was most important as a test of bravery. In Indian warfare, killing an enemy was not as important as showing valor. The greatest act of bravery was to come into contact with the enemy and touch him. The French trappers who saw this practice called it counting *coup*. Most braves—young Indian warriors—carried special sticks with which to count *coup*. The more *coups* the brave had, the higher his place in the tribe. Other acts won recognition for the brave. Among some tribes, for instance, rescuing a wounded warrior was considered more valorous than killing an enemy.

Between war and the buffalo hunt, the Plains Indians lived in small, scattered groups. But every year or so, these groups would gather for the Sun Dance. The aim of the Sun Dance was to bring visions and dreams to its dancers. The Sun Dancers fasted for days, staring all the while at a sacred object, usually a buffalo skull, which represented the sun. At the end, a warrior might be rewarded with a vision of victory in battle or of some other event. The Sun Dance was the great religious ceremony for the "People of Dreams," as one historian has called the Plains Indians.

Foremost among the "people of dreams" were the Dakotas, whose name means "league of friends." Whites called them the Sioux. For hundreds of years most Sioux lived in the forests of what is now Minnesota, where they lived by farming. With the coming of the horse, they abandoned their villages to move west. There they joined the western, or Teton, and central, or Yankton, groups.

At the close of the eighteenth century, the Sioux numbered about 30,000 people. By then they had become the most renowned warriors on the Plains. With their allies, the Cheyenne and the Arapaho, they hunted, made war, and traveled the Plains as a free, proud people. But this glorious time was to last for less than half a century, for in the early 1800s white men—whom the Sioux called *wasichu*—arrived on the Plains.

Tough, resourceful French fur trappers—the Voyageurs—had been in contact with the Plains tribes throughout the 1700s. After the Louisiana Purchase of 1803 added the Plains region to the United States, Americans came. These men, who trapped beaver for its highly valued fur, became the legendary mountain men. They got along well with most tribes, often marrying Indian women. But by the 1830s, the beaver were gone from the streams of the Plains and the Rockies. Then, for the first time, large groups of white people arrived on the Plains. They were emi-

A nineteenth-century engraving depicts Sioux Indians.

grants, traveling overland to the Oregon Country.

This was the first major contact between whites and Plains Indians, and the Indians reacted with mixed emotions. There were occasional attacks on wagon trains, but the image of a circle of wagons surrounded by howling Indians is mostly a myth created by Hollywood. The emigrants were traveling through the Plains, not settling on it. The Indians were angered when travelers cut down precious groves of cottonwood trees, or hunted the buffalo, but they were not usually hostile to white emigrants.

They continued to fight each other, however. The 1830s and 1840s were a time of constant warfare between many

Trappers and hunters like the one shown above were among the first whites to explore the Plains.

Plains tribes. The fighting made the Plains unsafe for white travelers. The government sent army troops up the Missouri River and into the Plains. In the 1840s, several trading posts were converted to forts. Still, the troops—whom the Indians called "long knives," after their swords—were there to try to keep peace among the tribes, not to fight them. The Plains were still considered a desert, rich in buffalo hides perhaps, but not worth settling.

The arrival of the whites brought the Indians things that were both useful and terrible. The Indians traded hides for metal tools and utensils, and for guns, which made hunting even easier. But the whites brought an unseen but deadly enemy with them—disease. Epidemic disease was almost unknown among the Indians before the nineteenth century. But as more whites arrived, epidemics of smallpox, measles, and other diseases ravaged many tribes. In 1837, one tribe, the Mandan, was almost completely wiped out in a few weeks by smallpox. The whites also brought liquor to the Plains. The Indians had even less experience with alcohol than with disease. Traders found they could coax bargains out of the Indians by treating them to very cheap,

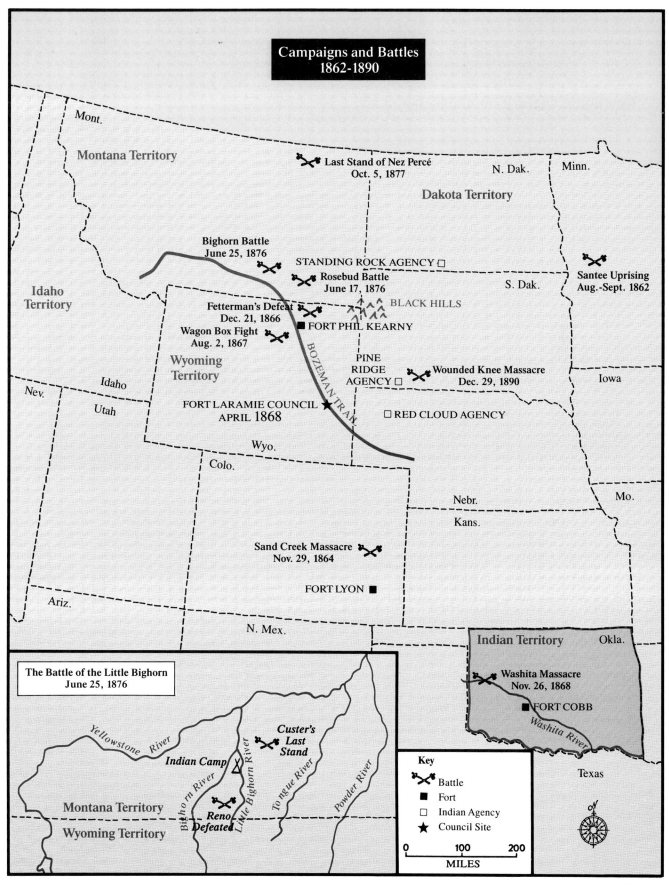

Campaigns and Battles 1862-1890

Montana Territory
Mont.

Last Stand of Nez Percé
Oct. 5, 1877

N. Dak.   Minn.

Dakota Territory

Bighorn Battle
June 25, 1876

STANDING ROCK AGENCY ☐

Rosebud Battle
June 17, 1876

S. Dak.

Santee Uprising
Aug.-Sept. 1862

Idaho
Territory

Fetterman's Defeat
Dec. 21, 1866

BLACK HILLS

Wagon Box Fight
Aug. 2, 1867

FORT PHIL KEARNY

Wyoming
Territory

PINE
RIDGE
AGENCY ☐

Wounded Knee Massacre
Dec. 29, 1890

Iowa

Idaho

BOZEMAN TRAIL

Nev.
Utah

FORT LARAMIE COUNCIL
APRIL 1868

★

☐ RED CLOUD AGENCY

Wyo.

Colo.

Nebr.

Mo.

Kans.

Sand Creek Massacre
Nov. 29, 1864

Ariz.

FORT LYON ■

N. Mex.

Indian Territory   Okla.

Washita Massacre
Nov. 26, 1868

■ FORT COBB

Washita River

The Battle of the Little Bighorn
June 25, 1876

Yellowstone River

Custer's
Last
Stand

Indian Camp

Reno
Defeated

Bighorn River

Little Bighorn River

Tongue River

Powder River

Montana Territory
Wyoming Territory

Texas

Key
✕ Battle
■ Fort
☐ Indian Agency
★ Council Site

0   100   200
MILES

17

almost poisonous whisky. Alcohol made some Indians forget their traditional way of life, making them dependent on often dishonest whites.

Another group of people began arriving in the Plains. They were eastern Indians—Cherokee, Choctaw, Delaware, and other tribes. For two centuries, white settlers had been moving west from the eastern seacoast. The Native Americans who lived in these regions had often resisted the tide of settlement, but frequent warfare, along with disease, had weakened their numbers. In the early nineteenth century, many whites were demanding that Indian lands in the South be opened to settlement. In 1830, during Andrew Jackson's presidency, Congress passed the Indian Removal Act. This law stated that the government could take Indian lands as long as compensation was given. Even though the Supreme Court had ruled that such forced removal was unconstitutional, thousands of Indians were uprooted in the 1830s and 1840s and sent to the "lands reserved for the Indians" west of the Mississippi River. The best-known removal took place in 1838, when the U.S. Army relocated the peaceful, agricultural Cherokee Indians from Georgia to what is now Oklahoma. Some 4,000 people died on this "Trail of Tears." Though they did not immediately realize it, much the same fate awaited the Plains Indians.

In 1849, gold was discovered in California. The stream of whites crossing the Plains swelled to a flood. Indian attacks on emigrants increased as travelers consumed the wood, water, and game that the Indians depended on for survival. Washington decided that something had to be done.

In 1846, the U.S. government had appointed a special United States Indian Agent: Tom Fitzpatrick, a veteran mountain man the Indians called "Broken Hand" because of an old injury. In September 1851, Fitzpatrick called a great council at Horse Creek, near Fort Laramie, an army post on the North Platte River in what is now the state of Wyoming.

Representatives of almost all the Plains tribes poured into Horse Creek—Cheyenne and Sioux, Arapaho and Crow, Shoshone and Assiniboine. A few tribes, such as the Pawnee and Comanche, did not attend. But within weeks about 12,000 Indians, the largest such gathering in the history of the Plains, had arrived at Horse Creek. To keep order, there were 300 U.S. soldiers—very nervous soldiers, for some of the tribes at the council were bitter enemies.

The purpose of the council was to bring a general peace to the Plains. The Indians agreed to halt their warfare and not to bother the whites. In return, the whites agreed to protect the Indians from attacks by whites. The Indians also received a cash payment of $50,000 a year.

But the Horse Creek agreements—like agreements before and after them—were worthless. Some Indians refused to honor them, because they did not support the tribal representative who

This drawing shows a group of Sioux at the Horse Creek conference of 1851.

signed them. Whites liked to deal with Indian "chiefs," but many chiefs were religious or military leaders who did not speak for all their people. The peace lasted barely three years.

In 1854, on a spot just a few miles from Horse Creek, a Sioux killed a cow from a wagon train. He had thought the cow had been abandoned, but the cow's owner angrily demanded $25. The Indian didn't have the money, so the emigrant took his case to the army at Fort Laramie.

A foolhardy young officer decided to take matters into his own hands. Gathering a handful of volunteers—and two cannons—Second Lieutenant J. J. Grattan marched out of Fort Laramie and into the Sioux camp. The Sioux elders tried to convince him that payment would be made. Grattan either misunderstood his interpreter or chose to ignore the Sioux's assurances. He ordered his men to fire their cannons into the Sioux camp. The Sioux attacked, and within minutes the lieutenant and all his men were dead.

When newspapers in the East published reports of the "massacre" of Grattan and his troops, people called for revenge. Even though the officers at Fort Laramie told their superiors that the incident was due to Grattan's foolishness, the government sent more troops to the Plains. In 1855, Colonel W. S. Harney, a veteran of fighting against the Seminole Indians in Florida, arrived in the area. He conducted a one-sided campaign that restored peace at the cost of many Indian lives.

The fighting in the 1850s began a conflict that would last, on and off, for over three decades. The Sioux and their allies were now the bitter enemies of the whites. But the next phase of the conflict would take place not on the Plains but in the wooded lands of western Minnesota.

2

FIRE ON THE PLAINS

In April 1861, the Civil War started. Most of the Regular Army soldiers left the Plains and were replaced by poorly trained volunteers. Yet, apart from a few incidents, the first year of the war brought a kind of peace to the Plains. With the coming of the war, fewer of the white people appeared. The soldiers were gone. Tribes hunted and fought their traditional enemies again. But in the summer of 1862, whites and Indians would again be at war.

The Santee Sioux lived in western Minnesota. Unlike their High Plains relatives, they were a settled, farming people who lived mostly in wooded areas. In the decade before the Civil War, many whites had settled in the Santee's homeland. The Santee signed misleading treaties with government officials. By 1860, they had lost 90 percent of their traditional land.

Thirty-eight Sioux were hung at Mankato, Minnesota, in December 1862.

The Santee were supposed to receive annual payments in cash and food in return for their land. But in the early 1860s, the payments stopped coming. Faced with starvation, the Santee appealed to traders and Indian Agents (government officials who "managed" Indian affairs). They refused to give the Indians supplies unless they had the money to pay for them. Many of the agents were incompetent and corrupt, and many of the traders were downright cruel. When Little Crow, one of the major Santee leaders, asked trader Andrew Myrick for credit to buy food, Myrick told him the Indians "could eat grass for all I care." Western Minnesota was like a powder keg ready to explode. The spark came on August 17.

Four hungry young Indian men had been looking for food that afternoon. One of them found some eggs. The others warned him against taking them. The eggs belonged to a white farmer, and the Indians might get in trouble. The brave who found the eggs boasted

Little Crow of the Santee Sioux.

he was not afraid of the whites. To prove it, he killed the farmer and his family.

Little Crow was angry when he heard of the incident. He knew the whites would retaliate against the Santee. Some of his warriors wanted to attack the settlers first. Little Crow argued with them. "You are fools," he told those who wanted war. "Your eyes are full of smoke." Little Crow had tried to cooperate with the whites—he even wore store-bought clothes and had become a Christian. But when a brave called him a coward, he agreed to fight.

The next morning, 2,000 Santee warriors rose up against whites throughout the valley of the Minnesota River. Farms and villages were burned. Some 400 settlers were killed, hundreds more were taken prisoner, and 30,000 whites fled in panic. The Indians had their revenge against the traders. Andrew Myrick's body was found with his mouth stuffed full of grass. Some whites who had treated the Indians fairly, though, were not harmed.

The Santee uprising, like countless other clashes between whites and Indians, had its roots in white mistrust and prejudice. White culture and Indian culture were very different, and most whites thought the Indians were "inferior." To whites, the Indians were at best an obstacle to settlement, and at worst, dangerous "savages." Matters were made worse by the government's habit of breaking treaties whenever it was convenient to do so. The Santee had been mistrusted, discriminated against, and lied to by the government and the settlers. The uprising was not just an outbreak of violence, but one people's fight for existence.

After a few days, a handful of settlers managed to drive the Indians back. But the uprising did not end until 1,600 soldiers under General Henry H. Sibley arrived on September 19. Sibley's force defeated the Santee and rescued the white captives. Then he persuaded many Santee to surrender. Those that did were arrested and tried for their crimes. The average "trial" lasted five minutes. When Sibley's makeshift court was finished, 303 Indians were sentenced to death.

Word of the sentences reached President Abraham Lincoln. He ordered an investigation. An army officer stationed at St. Paul reported to the president, "I feel confident that if all the Indian outbreaks upon this continent were carefully examined and honestly probed to the bottom, the whole cause and origin would be found in the thievish and dishonest conduct of the government agency officers and traders." Lincoln commuted the sentences of all but 38 prisoners. On a cold December morning, the 38 were hanged at Mankato, Minnesota. It was the largest execution in American history. A year after the uprising, Little Crow, who had escaped the soldiers, was shot down in a farmer's field.

The surviving Santee fled to the Plains. Even those who had not taken part in the uprising were banished to a dismal reservation in the Dakota Territory. A young Hunkpapa Sioux was among those who visited the exiled Santee and listened to their stories. His name was Tatanka Yotanka. Whites would come to know him as Sitting Bull.

Conflict spread to the southern Plains, where the Southern Cheyenne lived in Colorado. They had an able

Santee attack the town of New Ulm, Minnesota, in the uprising of 1862.

ATTENTION!
INDIAN
FIGHTERS

Having been authorized by the Governor to raise a Company of 100 day

U. S. VOL CAVALRY!

For immediate service against hostile Indians. I call upon all who wish to engage in such service to call at my office and enroll their names immediately.

Pay and Rations the same as other U. S. Volunteer Cavalry.

Parties furnishing their own horses will receive 40c per day, and rations for the same, while in the service.

The Company will also be entitled to all horses and other plunder taken from the Indians.

Office first door East of Recorder's Office.

HAL. SAYR.

Central City, Aug. 13, '64.

chief, Black Kettle, who wanted to live peacefully with the white settlers. In 1864, Black Kettle and 700 Cheyenne made camp at Sand Creek, near the Fort Lyon army post in eastern Colorado.

On November 29, 1864, dawn broke over Sand Creek. A white flag, symbolizing Black Kettle's desire for peace, flew over the Cheyenne camp.

The white flag was ignored by the 750 men of the Colorado Militia who stormed into the village. The militiamen, led by John M. Chivington, a former minister, killed men, women, and children alike. Black Kettle escaped with some Cheyenne, although his wife and 300 others were killed.

Chivington's raid made him a hero to many Colorado settlers. But the army and many other Americans were shocked at the unprovoked massacre. Chivington managed to escape punishment, even though a congressional committee reported that the Sand Creek massacre "scarcely has its parallel in the annals of Indian barbarity."

The remaining Southern Cheyenne went on the warpath, cutting a trail of destruction as they moved north. In 1865, they arrived in the Powder River country of Wyoming, where many Northern Cheyenne, Sioux, and Arapaho were gathered. Among these Indians were the remarkable chiefs who would lead their people against the whites in the years ahead—chiefs like Red Cloud, Sitting Bull, and Crazy Horse. The Cheyenne's story of Chivington's treachery, like the Santee's before it, fueled the Plains people's fears of white expansion. The Cheyenne and their allies smoked the war pipe. They pledged to defend their land. But in the years ahead, more and more white people came to the Plains, and the whites' hunger for land would lead to constant conflict.

In the spring of 1865, the Civil War ended. The Regular Army returned to the West. The army was small and poorly equipped, and it suffered from desertion and poor morale. But it was led by Civil War veterans like Generals William Sherman and Philip Sheridan—tough, seasoned fighters who were determined to subdue the Indians, whatever the cost.

The Plains were changing rapidly. Previously, the region had been considered a "land bridge" between the settled, eastern region and the new lands on the west coast. But in the 1860s, whites began to settle on the Plains themselves.

In 1862, Congress had passed the Homestead Act. The law gave 160 acres of Plains land to settlers who farmed it for five years. Thousands of European immigrants, Civil War veterans, and freed slaves moved west to homestead. The old idea of the Plains as a desert finally died. Settlers were lured west by promises of fertile land. The reality was far different. The almost treeless and

This poster was used to recruit volunteer cavalry in Colorado, like the regiment commanded by Henry M. Chivington at Sand Creek.

THE BUFFALO SOLDIERS

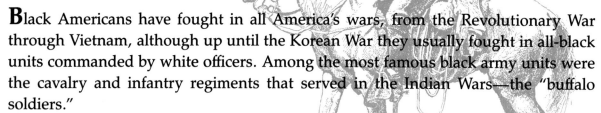

A buffalo soldier, as drawn by Frederic Remington.

Black Americans have fought in all America's wars, from the Revolutionary War through Vietnam, although up until the Korean War they usually fought in all-black units commanded by white officers. Among the most famous black army units were the cavalry and infantry regiments that served in the Indian Wars—the "buffalo soldiers."

In 1866, General Ulysses S. Grant ordered two black cavalry units, the Ninth and Tenth regiments, formed for service in the West. Later, the army raised two black infantry regiments, the 24th and 25th.

The Plains Indians first called the black troopers "buffalo soldiers." How they got the nickname is uncertain. According to some sources, the Indians believed the black soldiers' hair looked like buffalo fur. Others say the name came from the thick buffalo robes the soldiers wore during the cold Plains winters.

However the name came about, the buffalo soldiers saw long, hard service in the West. The Ninth battled Apache in Texas and New Mexico in the 1870s and 1880s and helped put down the Ghost Dance uprising in 1890. The Tenth was stationed in Kansas during the late 1860s. In the 1870s, the regiment fought Comanche in and around the Indian Territory. From 1885 to 1886, the Tenth helped defeat the Apaches in Arizona. Both cavalry units went on to win distinction in the Spanish-American War of 1898.

Despite the buffalo soldiers' fine reputation, many white officers refused to serve with them. One exception was Lieutenant John J. Pershing, who led a troop of the Tenth Cavalry in the 1890s. He later commanded the American Expeditionary Force in Europe during World War I. His high praise for the buffalo soldiers earned him the nickname "Black Jack."

Black troopers usually got older horses and weapons than whites, and the army awarded them far fewer promotions and medals. Despite this unfairness, the buffalo soldiers had a lower desertion rate and higher morale than many all-white units.

The buffalo soldiers added an important page to America's military history. Their proud service continued a tradition that lasts till this day.

waterless Plains were difficult to farm. The 160 acres offered by the government could barely support a family. Many would-be farmers "went bust" and moved back east. But others stayed. In the 1870s, immigrants from Russia arrived. Many were Mennonites (a religious sect) of German ancestry. They brought with them strains of the tough red wheat they had grown on the Plains-like steppes of Russia. This wheat proved perfect for the Plains. Eventually, the region would become the breadbasket of America and the world.

Others sought wealth through cattle.

In the 1860s, cowboys began to herd hardy longhorn cattle north from Texas through the Plains. The cattle were driven to boom towns like Cheyenne, Wyoming, and Abilene, Kansas, where they were loaded aboard trains and shipped to the slaughterhouses of Chicago. When barbed wire was invented in 1873, huge ranches sprang up on the Plains.

But nothing spurred the settlement of the Plains more than the railroad. By the late 1860s, a web of tracks had begun moving west through land once inhabited only by the Indians and buffalo. The railroads encouraged settlement,

The coming of the railroad brought almost total extinction to the great buffalo herds of the Plains.

because the government gave huge grants of land to railroad companies. The railroads allowed army troops to be moved quickly from one trouble spot to another. The trains also brought buffalo hunters to the Plains. Rich easterners and European noblemen organized buffalo-hunting expeditions much as they would go on African safaris. They and the professional buffalo hunters killed millions of the animals for their hides, leaving the carcasses to rot. In some areas the stench of rotting meat hung in the air for miles around. By the 1870s, the buffalo, on which the Plains Indians depended for survival, were on their way to near extermination. The Indians watched in dismay as the "iron horse" and its tracks cut through their lands, leaving a trail of slaughtered buffalo, rowdy settlements, and army posts in its wake.

The next great conflict on the Plains, however, would be fought not over a railroad but over a wagon road.

In 1865, the army sent a force under Patrick O'Connor to the Powder River country. The troopers were to "pacify" the Sioux, Cheyenne, and Arapaho in the region. O'Connor's expedition got lost and almost starved to death. After this failure, Washington decided to negotiate with the Indians rather than fight. They sent a delegation to the Powder River with a treaty. According to its terms, The Indians would be allowed to remain in the region, but they were to let the army build several forts in the area. The forts were needed to protect the Bozeman Trail.

The Bozeman Trail, named for miner John Bozeman, who surveyed it, ran 500 miles from Julesburg, Colorado, to gold mines near Virginia City, Montana. Before the Bozeman Trail was laid out, supplies for the miners had to travel a difficult route from Idaho. Unfortunately, the trail ran through the Sioux's favorite hunting grounds. A few minor chiefs had signed the treaty, but none of the Sioux's respected leaders "touched the pen." The Sioux grew resentful as hundreds of wagons began passing through their land. When 700 soldiers arrived at Fort Laramie, the Sioux realized they had been misled. In 1866, the Sioux and their allies went on the warpath. The two-year conflict that followed is usually called Red Cloud's War, after the Sioux chief who led the Indian forces.

Mahpina Luta, or Red Cloud, was about forty years old when war broke out. An able leader and fierce warrior, he was said to be "as full of action as a tiger." His opponent was General Henry B. Carrington. Carrington began building three forts to protect the trail. Work had scarcely begun when Red Cloud and his braves began attacking the soldiers.

On December 21, 1866, a "wood train" of wagons left Fort Phil Kearny near Piney Creek, Wyoming. The soldiers were gathering wood when they came under attack. They signaled the fort for help. Carrington quickly ordered a force to relieve the wood train. Captain William J. Fetterman asked to command it.

Carrington was reluctant to let Fetterman lead the relief force. The arrogant young officer didn't think much of the Indians. A few days before he had bragged, "Give me eighty men and I'll ride through the entire Sioux nation." But Fetterman was the senior officer. Carrington gave him command but ordered him to do nothing but relieve the wood train. Under no circumstances was he to go beyond Lodge Pole Ridge, a few miles away. Ironically, when Fetterman rode through Fort Phil Kearny's gates, exactly eighty troopers rode behind him.

The Indians broke off the attack before Fetterman's force could reach the wood train. The wood train soldiers made it back to the fort. But Fetterman didn't turn back. He saw a few Indian horsemen just below the ridge. Fetterman knew he would be disobeying orders if he pursued them, but he couldn't resist the opportunity. With a whoop, he spurred his horse into a gallop. The cavalrymen charged the ridge.

Fetterman was about to become a victim of the Indians' favorite tactic—ambush. The warriors below the ridge, led by a fierce young Oglala Sioux named Crazy Horse, were a decoy force. When Fetterman reached the top of the ridge, he was met by about two thousand warriors under Red Cloud. Within minutes, Fetterman and his command were wiped out. It was the Indians' greatest victory thus far.

When the harsh Plains winter arrived, the Indians returned to their villages, only to resume fighting in the

Red Cloud and his granddaughter, Burning Heart.

spring. Encouraged by Fetterman's defeat, Red Cloud sought another major battle.

On August 2, 1867, Red Cloud and a thousand warriors attacked another wood train. This time the bluecoats had the advantage. They crouched below the sides of their wagon boxes, which protected them from the Indians' arrows—giving the battle its name, the Wagon Box Fight. The soldiers also had fast-firing breech-loading rifles. The Indians retreated after losing about 200

The Wagon Box Fight: Bluecoats crouch in their wagons, firing on Red Cloud's circling warriors.

braves. The soldiers had casualties of five men.

Neither the Fetterman Massacre nor the Wagon Box Fight was a decisive victory. Red Cloud's warriors continued attacking the forts and travelers on the Bozeman Trail. But the government decided to abandon the forts and the trail. The railroad had reached Wyoming, making it easier to ship supplies to the Montana mines.

In April 1868, a peace commission arrived at Fort Laramie. They drafted a treaty that guaranteed the Powder River region—including the sacred Black Hills of South Dakota—to the Indians. Red Cloud and his allies found the terms acceptable and touched the pen. A few

months later, the troopers hauled down the flag at Fort Phil Kearny. They had barely marched away when a party of joyful Sioux set the hated fort on fire.

Red Cloud's War was a victory for the Indians. But like all the Indians' successes, it was short-lived. Within a decade, the Fort Laramie Treaty would be violated and the Sioux would be locked in a death struggle with the U.S. Army. The seeds for that conflict, which climaxed at the Little Bighorn River in 1876, were sown in Red Cloud's War.

But Red Cloud never fought again. He and his followers accepted settlement on a reservation in South Dakota, where he lived until his death in 1909. Red Cloud encouraged his people to live in peace, and he opposed the war-like activities of Sitting Bull and Crazy Horse. With dignity and eloquence, he now used his voice, rather than a weapon, to promote his people's cause. In 1870, he traveled to New York and spoke before a great crowd at the Cooper Union School:

> I am a representative of the original American race, the first people of this continent. We are good and not bad. We have given you nearly all our land, and if we had any more land to give we would be glad to give it. We have nothing more. We are driven into a very little land, and we want you now, as our dear friends, to help us with the government of the United States.

But the Plains were still the scene of bitter battles. After Red Cloud's War, the fighting again shifted south, this time to Indian Territory, the present state of Oklahoma.

Amazingly, Black Kettle and his followers still tried to live in peace with the whites, even after Sand Creek. In the fall of 1868, Black Kettle moved to the Washita River in Indian Territory. Unfortunately for Black Kettle and his band, other Cheyenne had recently gone on the warpath in Kansas. The soldiers in nearby Fort Cobb were in no mood to trust Black Kettle. On the morning of November 26, 1868, soldiers stormed Black Kettle's camp in a repeat

The Fort Laramie treaty conference, 1868. General William Sherman is seated third from left.

This painting, Attack at Dawn, *depicts an action much like Custer's attack on Black Kettle's village on the Washita River.*

of Sand Creek. This time, Black Kettle was killed.

The troops who wiped out Black Kettle were commanded by Lieutenant Colonel George Armstrong Custer. He was a soldier destined to become one of the most controversial figures in the history of the Plains.

Custer was born in Ohio in 1839. In 1861, he graduated from West Point (last in his class), just in time for the Civil War. Young Lieutenant Custer quickly gained a reputation as a coura-

geous cavalry commander. He was promoted directly to brigadier general after his first charge. General George McClellan, his commander, called him "a reckless, gallant boy, undeterred by fatigue, unconscious of fear." By the war's end he held a major general's rank.

After the war, Custer dabbled in business and considered a career in politics. But soon he returned to the army as a captain (he had been a "brevet" general, an officer promoted on the battlefield but without permanent

George Custer as a West Point cadet.

rank). He took command of the Seventh Cavalry Regiment at Fort Riley, Kansas, in July 1866. His early career in the West was checkered. He became known as a brave, if not particularly skillful, Indian fighter. He was also arrogant and stubborn. On one occasion he was relieved of his command after leaving his troops to visit his wife. But Custer had influential friends, including General Philip Sheridan, who restored him to duty. Custer also had a great flair for the dramatic. On horseback, with his long blond hair flowing in the wind, ivory-handled pistols strapped to his hip, he seemed the very model of a dashing cavalry officer. Custer's magazine articles and a book, *My Life on the Plains* (which one of his officers liked to call *My Lie on the Plains*), added to his reputation. He was already well known when, in 1874, he was ordered to lead an exploring expedition to the Black Hills of the Dakota Territory.

3

"TODAY IS A GOOD DAY TO DIE!"

The Sioux watched from the craggy rocks as the spectacle unrolled before them. A hundred wagons rolled through the valley below, their canvas tops white as sails against the blue summer sky. A thousand blue-coated soldiers rode alongside the wagons. There was even a band on horseback. They played an old Irish drinking song, "Garryowen," which the Seventh Cavalry Regiment, U.S. Army, had made its theme. It was the summer of 1874, and George Custer had arrived in the Black Hills of the Dakota Territory.

The Black Hills rise hundreds of feet from the surrounding plains in stark, rocky formations. This unusual place meant much to the people of the Plains. The Black Hills were *Paha Sapa*—the sacred ground. The dead were laid to rest there, and their spirits were believed to dwell among the peaks. The Sioux also

Custer's wagon train, photographed from a Black Hills peak in the summer of 1874.

valued the hills for their abundant game and for the tall pine trees that made fine tipi poles.

The U.S. government had recognized the Indians' right to the Black Hills in the Fort Laramie Treaty of 1868. That document guaranteed the region, and much of the Powder River country, to the Indians. When the Sioux gathered, they angrily wondered what Custer—whom they called Long Hair—was doing in the Black Hills.

Custer was looking for gold. For years there had been rumors of gold in the area, and when Custer's scientists tested the soil, they did find traces of the mineral. Custer sent a scout back with a message: "There is gold in the grassroots!"

Custer's report touched off a gold rush. Within weeks, an army of fortune-hunters headed into the Sioux's sacred ground. Old-timers warned the "Black Hillers" of danger from the Indians. "I'd rather be scalped than poor" was the

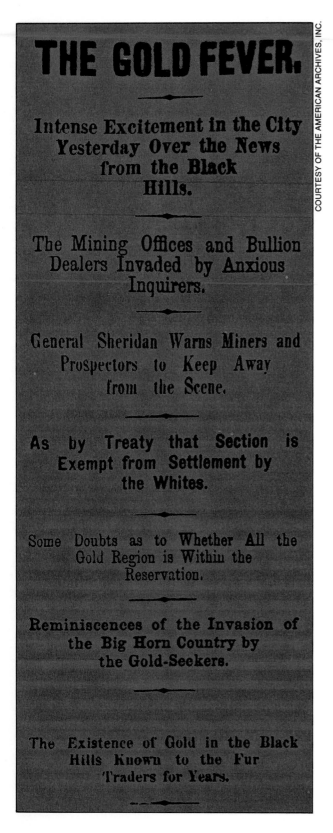

THE GOLD FEVER.

Intense Excitement in the City Yesterday Over the News from the Black Hills.

The Mining Offices and Bullion Dealers Invaded by Anxious Inquirers.

General Sheridan Warns Miners and Prospectors to Keep Away from the Scene.

As by Treaty that Section is Exempt from Settlement by the Whites.

Some Doubts as to Whether All the Gold Region is Within the Reservation.

Reminiscences of the Invasion of the Big Horn Country by the Gold-Seekers.

The Existence of Gold in the Black Hills Known to the Fur Traders for Years.

usual reply. The Sioux bitterly named Custer's route the Thieves' Road.

According to the Fort Laramie Treaty, the Black Hills and the surrounding area were "unceded territory"—the Indians' own land. The treaty had also created a reservation for the Sioux in the Dakota Territory, where they could settle and receive government rations from Indian agencies. Some Indians did move onto the reservation, but others preferred the free life on the Plains. The government considered the "agency" Indians peaceful. The non-reservation Sioux were classified as "hostile."

Actually, the difference between "hostile" and "agency" Indians existed mostly in the government's imagination. Many "agency" Indians lived on the reservation throughout the winter but moved west to hunt in the summer. In turn, many "hostile" bands drew rations at the agencies during the cold weather.

Some Indian leaders, however, refused to have anything to do with the reservation. They wanted only to live as they had before the white people had come—although that was becoming difficult as the railroad advanced and the buffalo disappeared. "You are fools to make yourselves slaves to a piece of fat bacon, some hard-tack and a little coffee and sugar," said the foremost of these leaders—Sitting Bull—to the agency Sioux.

The August 28, 1874, Chicago Inter Ocean *describes the Black Hills gold rush.*

Sitting Bull, a Sioux of the Hunkpapa band, was about forty years old in 1874. He was respected throughout the Plains for his accomplishments as a statesman and spiritual leader. His ally was Crazy Horse, the fierce warrior who had fought with Red Cloud. Now in his early thirties, Crazy Horse was chief of the Oglala Sioux band. Like Sitting Bull, he was determined to save the old way of life.

The Black Hills gold rush put the army in an awkward position. The gold seekers were trespassers, but the army didn't have the manpower to keep them away. The Indians grew angrier and attacks on whites increased.

At first the government offered to buy the Black Hills. Washington offered the Indians only $6 million. (The Black Hills eventually yielded half a billion dollars in gold dust.) Sitting Bull was asked if he would agree to a sale. He reached down and scooped up a handful of soil. "I would not sell as much as this," he said. Most of the other chiefs agreed with him. As the new year of 1875 approached, Washington decided the only solution was to call out the army to subdue the so-called "hostiles."

On December 3, 1875, runners left the agencies bearing a message for the Plains Sioux and Cheyenne: All Indians had to be on the reservation by January 31 or the army would be sent after them.

It was a ridiculous demand to make in the dead of winter. "It was very cold, and many of our people and ponies

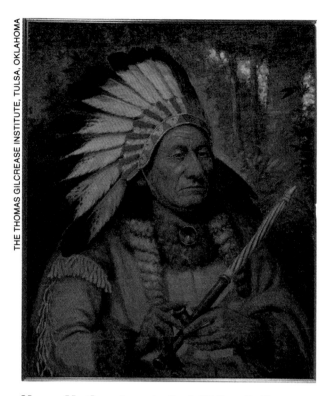

Henry H. Cross's portrait of Sitting Bull captures the chief's strength and determination.

would have died in the snow. Also, we were in our own country and were doing no harm," a young Oglala Sioux man said later. When the deadline came, only a few Indians had arrived at the agencies.

On February 7, the Department of the Interior (which had control over Indian matters) turned the matter over to the army. Immediately, army commanders began planning a winter campaign.

Winter fighting was a favorite army strategy. A swift cavalry strike against a snowbound Indian village could be devastating. Unfortunately for the army, the winter of 1875–76 was harsh even by Plains standards. Snow and cold kept braves and bluecoats alike confined to camp. It was not until March that the first cavalrymen under General George Reynolds set out from Fort Fetterman.

On the bitterly cold night of March 16, Reynolds' troopers attacked a Sioux village on Clear Creek, a Powder River tributary. The village was quickly captured. It looked as though the first battle of this new conflict would be a victory for the army. The camp's leader, however, was Crazy Horse himself.

Crazy Horse quickly led his braves in a counterattack. The Sioux's arrows and bullets, combined with the intense cold, forced Reynolds and his men to make a fast retreat. The first victory of the campaign went to the Sioux.

News of Crazy Horse's victory spread through the Sioux like wildfire. As the weather grew warm, many Indian bands joined forces with Crazy Horse and Sitting Bull. By June, about two thousand people were camped along the Rosebud River.

For the Indians it was a glorious time. All the bands of the Sioux were represented in the great camp, along with plenty of Cheyenne. During the day there was hunting; at night, the sounds of feasting and dancing filled the air.

It was at the camp on the Rosebud that Sitting Bull performed a sun dance. He rose before dawn. As the sky lightened, a relative cut him fifty times on

A newspaper illustration showing the Rosebud fight.

each arm. Then, his face to the sun, he danced. Finally, he collapsed.

When Sitting Bull awoke he described his vision. He had seen blue-coated soldiers falling upside down into the Sioux camp. To Sitting Bull, this meant a great Indian victory lay ahead.

As the Sioux hunted and feasted, the army finally got moving. According to plan, General George Crook, a veteran Indian fighter fresh from a campaign against the Apache, was to approach from the north. General Alfred Terry would push west from Fort Lincoln in North Dakota. General John Gibbon would attack from the east. The goal was to trap the Sioux between the three columns.

On May 26, General Crook and 1,200 soldiers, plus 300 Crow and Shoshone Indians, set out from Fort Fetterman. On the morning of June 17, the column arrived in the valley of the Rosebud River. Suddenly the hills crackled with rifle fire. Shouting their war cries, a thousand braves led by Crazy Horse charged into the valley.

The pitched battle lasted more than two hours. Crook's cavalry charged again and again; the Indians drove them back. Crook ordered a withdrawal. The surviving bluecoats got away, largely because of the bravery of their Crow allies, who held off the Sioux and rescued a wounded officer.

After the battle, Sitting Bull was asked if his vision had been fulfilled. No, said Sitting Bull, the great battle was still to come.

The Rosebud Fight cheered the Indi-

ans. As news of the victory spread, even more people joined Sitting Bull. The village grew so large it had to be moved. The Indians struck their tipis and moved west, to the banks of a Montana Territory river that the Indians called the Greasy Grass. The whites called it the Little Bighorn.

Meanwhile, General Terry's column was on the march. Attached to it was the Seventh Cavalry under George Custer.

Ironically, Custer nearly missed the 1876 campaign. He had been in Washington that spring, called to testify before a congressional committee investigating corruption in the Bureau of Indian Affairs. Custer's testimony was unfavorable to W. W. Belknap, the Secretary of War—who also happened to be President Ulysses Grant's brother-in-law. Grant was furious with Custer and wanted to dismiss him from the army. Once again, Custer's influential friends rescued him, and on May 17 he rode out of Fort Abraham Lincoln in the Dakota Territory at the head of his regiment.

The column's line of march ran parallel to the Yellowstone River. A chartered steamboat, the *Far West*, accompanied the soldiers. On June 21, Custer and Terry met General Gibbon and his men. That night, the officers met aboard the *Far West*. Since there was no word from Crook, the other generals had no idea how many warriors they would be facing. Terry gave Custer and his fast-moving cavalry the job of finding the Indians' camp. Terry and Gibbon would follow with the slower infantry.

Custer (center) and his family and friends picnicked happily just weeks before the battle. Several of the men in this photograph were killed at the Little Bighorn.

The next morning the Seventh headed out. There were about six hundred officers and men in the regiment, including two of Custer's brothers, Tom and Boston. There were also some Crow Indian scouts; Isaiah Dorman, the regiment's black Indian-language interpreter; and a civilian correspondent. As they rode away, General Gibbon, knowing Custer's habit of recklessly charging into danger, called out, "Now Custer, don't be greedy! Wait for us."

"No, I will not," Custer shouted to his superior. Before Gibbon could reply, the Seventh was on its way.

On the morning of June 25, 1876, Crow scouts sighted an Indian encampment on the Little Bighorn. Realizing the regiment had probably been spotted by the Sioux already, Custer decided to act quickly. He gathered his officers to-

gether and outlined his plan. The Seventh would divide into three parts. One force, under Major Marcus Reno, would cross the Little Bighorn and attack from the west. Another force, commanded by Captain Frederick Benteen, would guard the mule train carrying the regiment's supplies and reinforce Reno. Custer would lead five troops of cavalry in an attack from the east. Custer probably hoped for a repeat of his victory at the Washita River eight years before.

The Sioux village on the Little Bighorn was not like the Cheyenne village on the Washita. It was probably the largest gathering of Indians ever on the Plains. There were at least three thousand people, including hundreds of warriors. Leading the braves were great war chiefs—Dull Knife and Two Moons of the Cheyenne, and Crazy Horse,

Gall, and Rain-in-the-Face among the Sioux—all inspired by Sitting Bull's leadership. But Custer did not know this. As the afternoon sun blazed down, the Seventh rode to the attack.

Reno's force was the first into combat. The troopers panicked at the sight of so many Indians and dismounted. Reno and his men managed to get behind a small ridge of earth, which gave them some cover, but the Indians' rifle fire proved too intense. As men fell around them, the troopers dashed back across the Little Bighorn to the relative safety of some bluffs. A short time later Benteen and his troopers joined them. There was no sign of Custer and his 215 men.

At about 3:00 P.M., Custer's force was atop a hill overlooking the valley of the Little Bighorn. Apart from women, children, and older people, the great village was deserted—the braves were off fighting Reno. Custer must have thought victory was in sight. Realizing he would need ammunition, he quickly scribbled a note for Captain Benteen:

> Benteen. Come on. Big village. Be quick. Bring Packs [of ammunition]. P.S. Bring Packs.

Custer handed the note to his orderly, an Italian immigrant named Giovanni Martini. Then he spurred his horse forward. Custer and his men began trotting toward the village. Giovanni Martini was the last white man to see Custer and live to tell the story.

A Sioux depiction of the Battle of the Little Bighorn.

Edgar Paxson's painting of the Battle of the Little Bighorn.

Hundreds of thousands of words have been written about the battle that followed, but the details of the fight are uncertain. The only surviving witnesses were the Sioux and Cheyenne. Often, their accounts contradicted each other, or changed over time. The only thing certain is that Custer and all his men died along the Little Bighorn.

If Custer had reached the village, the outcome of the battle might have been far different. But a handful of Cheyenne, realizing the danger to the village, distracted Custer. Others warned Sitting Bull and Crazy Horse of Custer's approach. While the troopers skirmished with the Cheyenne, the main body of warriors broke off the fight with Reno and charged at Custer's force.

It must have been a terrifying sight to the bluecoats—hundreds of shouting braves, painted and dressed for battle, charging on their swift ponies. Leading them was Crazy Horse. "Come on, Dakotas!" he shouted. "Today is a good day to fight. Today is a good day to die!"

Custer and his men tried to retreat, but it was impossible. The troopers forded the river and made it to a hilltop. According to some accounts, Custer was wounded in the crossing. Although artists have often portrayed Custer as being the last man to fall, his body was found on the hilltop. Scores of others lay around it.

The fight continued after Custer's death. The remaining soldiers tried to get away. All were cut down. Accounts of the last part of the battle differ. Sitting Bull once said that the whites had fought bravely. Other braves said they begged to be taken prisoner—none were—and that some killed themselves when they realized the situation was hopeless. But by all accounts it was a fierce battle. The fighting was so intense that some Indian bodies were found with their comrades' arrows in them.

An hour after it had begun, the battle was over. The braves rode back to continue the attack on Reno. As evening fell, their ammunition ran low. Sitting Bull and the other chiefs decided to break camp. The tipis were struck. By morning, the Indian bands had gone their separate ways.

The great summer of the Sioux was over.

The Indians leave the battleground after defeating Custer.

FROM THE LITTLE BIGHORN TO WOUNDED KNEE

On June 27, Terry and Gibbon arrived at the Little Bighorn. All that could be done was to send the wounded downriver in the *Far West* and bury the mutilated bodies of the dead. The only living thing on the battlefield was a horse, Comanche, that had belonged to one of Custer's officers. All 215 men of Custer's command had died, although seven bodies were never found. Fifty-seven of Reno's men had been killed.

In some ways, the Battle of the Little Bighorn—or Custer's Last Stand, as it was quickly dubbed—was a minor affair. Compared with the great battles of the Civil War, which had ended just a decade before, it was a mere skirmish. However, the fight sparked a controversy that has lasted into our own time.

Soldiers, writers, and armchair his-

The Sioux break camp after the battle. The title of this painting, Fruitless Victory, *sums up the result of the battle for the Indians.*

torians have long argued over the battle. The question they ask most often is, Why did Custer attack the great Sioux village immediately, rather than withdrawing and waiting for Terry and Gibbon? The answer will never be known, but it probably lies in Custer's personality. Custer thrived on glory. He was the kind of soldier who loves the charge and hates the slow, cautious advance. He may have been confident that his tough troopers would win even if outnumbered. Or he may simply have underestimated the strength of the Indian forces.

Some have charged that Custer rushed into battle to gain publicity for political purposes. According to two of his Crow scouts, Custer, like Sitting Bull, had had a vision before the battle. Custer told them that he would defeat the Sioux and then become the "Great Father" in Washington. The year 1876 was an election year. The Democratic

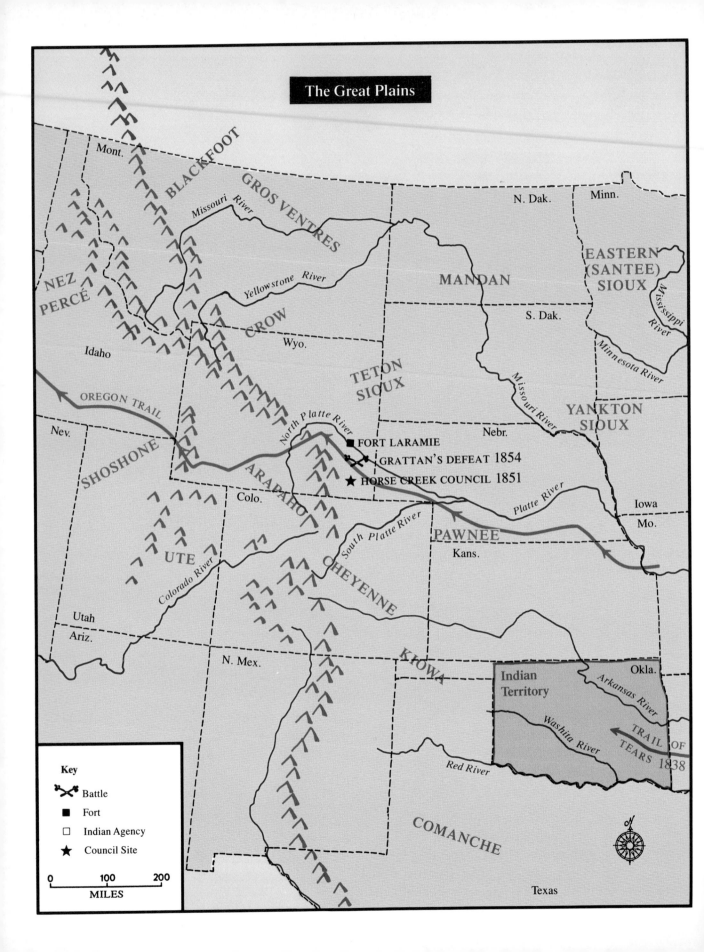

The Great Plains

Mont.

BLACKFOOT

GROS VENTRES

Missouri River

NEZ PERCÉ

Yellowstone River

CROW

Idaho

Wyo.

N. Dak.

Minn.

MANDAN

S. Dak.

EASTERN (SANTEE) SIOUX

Mississippi River

Minnesota River

TETON SIOUX

YANKTON SIOUX

Missouri River

OREGON TRAIL

Nev.

SHOSHONE

North Platte River

ARAPAHO

■ FORT LARAMIE

⚔ GRATTAN'S DEFEAT 1854

★ HORSE CREEK COUNCIL 1851

Nebr.

Platte River

Iowa

Mo.

Colo.

UTE

Colorado River

South Platte River

CHEYENNE

PAWNEE

Kans.

Utah

Ariz.

N. Mex.

KIOWA

Okla.

Arkansas River

Indian Territory

TRAIL OF TEARS 1838

Washita River

Red River

COMANCHE

Texas

Key

⚔ Battle

■ Fort

□ Indian Agency

★ Council Site

0   100   200

MILES

According to some accounts, Captain Myles Keogh's horse Comanche was the only living thing found on the Bighorn battlefield.

party, to which Custer belonged, met in St. Louis to choose its presidential candidate during the Bighorn campaign. Perhaps Custer hoped to end the campaign in a quick, spectacular victory and arrive at the convention to triumphantly accept his party's nomination. If so, he told no one but the scouts. Others have claimed Custer wanted to get the campaign over with quickly so he could attend the Centennial Exposition (a fair celebrating one hundred years of American independence) in Philadelphia.

One group, which included Custer's widow, felt that he had died because the rest of the regiment hadn't come to his aid. A court of inquiry held by the army uncovered some disturbing facts about Custer's leadership. The Seventh had

not been a happy regiment. The officers resented Custer's favoritism toward a "royal family" within the unit. (Seven of Custer's relatives served with the Seventh and all died at the Little Bighorn.) The enlisted men complained about his harsh—some said cruel—discipline. However, the court held Reno, Benteen, and the other surviving officers blameless for the defeat.

Many people believed the Indians hadn't won "fair and square." How could undisciplined braves defeat a trained, experienced cavalry regiment? The answer, according to one fantastic story, was that Sitting Bull had once attended West Point in disguise!

But the Native Americans had superior numbers and great leadership.

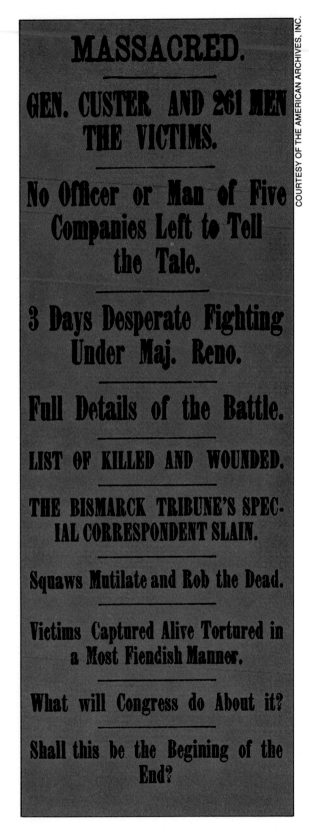

MASSACRED.

GEN. CUSTER AND 261 MEN THE VICTIMS.

No Officer or Man of Five Companies Left to Tell the Tale.

3 Days Desperate Fighting Under Maj. Reno.

Full Details of the Battle.

LIST OF KILLED AND WOUNDED.

THE BISMARCK TRIBUNE'S SPECIAL CORRESPONDENT SLAIN.

Squaws Mutilate and Rob the Dead.

Victims Captured Alive Tortured in a Most Fiendish Manner.

What will Congress do About it?

Shall this be the Begining of the End?

The Bismarck (Dakota Territory) Weekly Tribune describes the Bighorn battle. A Tribune reporter, Charles Kellog, was killed with Custer.

Their weapons were at least equal to those of the soldiers. Perhaps most important, they were fighting for the land and life they loved. Captain Benteen said, "We were at their hearths and homes—and they were fighting for all the good God gives anyone to fight for." When all is said and done, according to a modern historian, "Custer lost because the Indians won."

The Battle of the Little Bighorn was the Plains Indians' greatest victory, but it sealed their doom as a free people. When word of the fight reached the cities of the East—where Americans were happily celebrating the nation's centennial—the public went wild with shock and anger. *Massacred!* the newspaper headlines blared. "General Custer Killed. . . . The Entire Detachment Under His Command Slaughtered."

There was now no hope of negotiating with the Sioux for the Black Hills, or peacefully settling the conflict. The death of the popular Custer brought loud cries for revenge. The government, and most of the public, demanded that the "savages" be caught, punished, and confined to the reservations.

Even the Indians who had not been part of Sitting Bull's "hostiles" were punished. In July, all the western reservations were put under military control. Many agency Sioux were moved to reservations on the Missouri River, far from their traditional homeland. A month later, the government formally seized the Black Hills and the Powder River country from the Sioux, over the protests of Red Cloud and other leaders. The Sioux chief Spotted Tail said bitterly:

> This war did not spring up here in our land; this war was brought by the children of the Great Father [the soldiers] who came to take our land, and who do a great many evil things. . . . This war has come from robbery—from the stealing of our land.

But the bands of Sitting Bull, Crazy Horse, and their Cheyenne friends still roamed free.

More troops arrived in "hostile country" in the summer of 1876, but there were only a few minor fights. As fall approached, the army again planned a cold-weather campaign. This one was more successful than the last.

In October, a force under General Nelson Miles went after Sitting Bull, who was camped on the Tongue River. The Sioux avoided a major battle. One brave galloped into Miles's camp, leaving a note from the chief to the general, politely requesting him to leave some food and gunpowder and then go home.

A few days later Miles and Sitting

O. C. Seltzer painted the meeting between General Nelson Miles and Sitting Bull.

Bull met under a flag of truce. Through interpreters, Miles accused Sitting Bull of being an enemy to whites. Sitting Bull replied that he had no quarrel with the white people. He would quit fighting as soon as they left the Black Hills. Miles then asked him to surrender. Sitting Bull, knowing this would mean confinement on the reservation, replied, "The Great Spirit [God] made me an Indian—but not an agency Indian!" and left.

For the rest of the summer, Miles chased Sitting Bull through the Badlands of the Dakota Territory. Sitting Bull realized resistance was useless with winter coming on. There were just too many bluecoats. With two thousand followers, the great chief slipped across the border into Canada, where the soldiers couldn't follow.

Winter came early in 1876. In late November, snow fell in the valley of the Powder River, where the Sioux's Cheyenne allies had lived since the Custer fight. On November 25, soldiers made their way into the valley, looking for Crazy Horse's band. They found the Cheyenne instead and attacked. A few brave warriors held off the bluecoats until most of the village escaped. A terrible ordeal followed as the Cheyenne struggled through the cold and snow. Many died before they reached Crazy Horse's camp three days later, and most of the survivors gave themselves up at the agencies to get food.

By the new year, only Crazy Horse's band remained "on the loose." Pursuing Crazy Horse was the wily General George Crook. For months, Crazy Horse eluded Crook. It was not until April 1877 that the Oglala chief, low on ammunition and facing Crook's cannon, surrendered with his people at the Red Cloud agency.

Crazy Horse hated reservation life. But there was one consolation; he fell in love with, and married, a pretty Sioux girl. In September 1877, Crazy Horse's wife became sick. The Oglala chief rode beyond the agency's boundary to get a white doctor he had befriended. The agents thought he was trying to escape and sent soldiers after him. Crazy Horse was thrown into a jail cell. There was a scuffle, and Crazy Horse was stabbed to

Cheyenne of Dull Knife's band flee through the snow to Crazy Horse's camp.

LIBRARY OF CONGRESS

THE FLIGHT OF THE NEZ PERCÉ

Next to the Battle of the Little Bighorn, the Nez Percé campaign of 1877 is the best-known incident in the Indian Wars.

The Nez Percé lived in parts of what are now the states of Washington, Oregon, and Idaho. They were a peaceful people who boasted of their good relations with whites.

In 1877, however, white cattlemen began demanding the right to settle in the Wallowa Valley of Oregon, where a band of Nez Percé led by Chief Joseph lived. The government ordered the Nez Percé to move to a reservation in Idaho. Joseph refused. He tried to avoid bloodshed, but a few hotheaded young braves got in a fight with some white men. The army was sent in. In the Battle of White Bird Creek, the Nez Percé defeated an army unit, and the Nez Percé "war" began. Despite this victory, Joseph knew his band of about 500 people couldn't hope to defend the Wallowa Valley from the bluecoats for long. There was only one chance for freedom—to escape to Canada.

The journey that followed was a true epic. In four months, Joseph and his people walked about 1,700 miles across three major mountain ranges and countless rivers, streams, and canyons. Along the way, the Nez Percé skirmished more than twelve times with army columns. Joseph and his chiefs used their small force of about 100 warriors brilliantly. Joseph's military ability amazed army officers, who compared the chief's tactics to Napoleon's.

Then, a heartbreaking 30 miles from the Canadian border, the soldiers surrounded the Nez Percé. For six days the soldiers and the surviving braves fought in the Bear Paw Mountains of Montana. Finally, Joseph decided to surrender and save his people from cold and hunger. On October 5, 1877, he walked forward to meet the bluecoats. His eloquent surrender speech has become a classic:

> Our chiefs are dead. . . . It is cold and we have no blankets. My people, some of them, have run away to the hills, and have no blankets, no food. No one knows where they are—perhaps freezing to death. I want to have time to look for my children and see how many I can find. Maybe I shall find them among the dead. Hear me, my chiefs, I am tired. My heart is sick and sad. From where the sun now stands, I will fight no more forever.

Joseph and his band were sent to various reservations in the Indian Territory and Kansas. In 1904, Joseph died in Idaho, far from his beloved Wallowa Valley. "He died of a broken heart," his doctor said.

death. With his last words, the great warrior spoke of Custer. "All we wanted was to live in peace. . . . Then Long Hair came. They say we massacred him, but he would have done the same to us."

Canada offered Sitting Bull sanctuary but nothing more. Hunting was poor, but to return to the American territory would mean arrest. After five years, however, Sitting Bull decided to return to his ancestors' land. On July 18, 1881, he led his followers back across the border. The bluecoats were waiting. Silently, he handed his rifle to a young relative, who handed it to an officer. "Let it be known I was the last of my people to surrender my rifle," he said.

In 1883, the government moved Sitting Bull to the Standing Rock agency in South Dakota. He lived as far away from the agents as he could. But the Hunkpapa chief did have some dealings with the whites. In 1886, Sitting Bull toured with "Buffalo Bill" Cody's Wild West Show. He was very popular. People who had once howled for his blood now eagerly paid a dollar for his autograph. Sitting Bull, however, gave all the money away to the poor children he saw in the streets of the eastern cities.

By the end of the 1880s, the Sioux were at a low point. The buffalo were gone. They were living miserably on the reservations, surviving on the moldy

Sioux Indians performing the Ghost Dance.

bread and bacon that Sitting Bull had despised. Crazy Horse was dead, and Sitting Bull was practically a prisoner. The life they had once led was fast fading into memory. Then, from the west, came something that promised to restore the old ways. It was the Ghost Dance.

In 1888, there was an eclipse of the sun. When it was over, Wovoka, a Paiute Indian in Nevada, claimed to have received a vision. Wovoka—or Jack Wilson, as whites called him—said that a new era was coming for all the Indians. If they put aside their differences and danced in a circle, they would bring their ancestors back from the dead. These "ghosts" would make the whites disappear and the buffalo return. The old, free way of life would be restored. There would be peace and plenty for everyone.

Within a year the Ghost Dance religion had reached the Plains. It was eagerly accepted by the Sioux. But they added new elements to Wovoka's teaching. Wovoka and the earlier Ghost Dancers had stressed the religion's peaceful aspects. Some of the Sioux, however, believed that fighting the whites was an important part of the Ghost Dance. Sioux medicine men told braves that the dance would make them invincible in battle. Warriors painted Ghost Dance symbols on their shirts, hoping to make them bulletproof. By the winter of 1890, village after village had begun dancing.

The Ghost Dance terrified the Indian agents. They recalled the horrors of the Santee uprising almost thirty years before. Would the Ghost Dance lead to another uprising? "Indians are dancing in the snow and are wild and crazy," a South Dakota agent telegraphed to his superiors. "We need protection."

The U.S. government again sent in the army. Ironically, the unit ordered to the reservations of South Dakota was the Seventh Cavalry—Custer's old regiment.

The agents were the most concerned about Sitting Bull. The old chief still commanded the loyalty of many Sioux. If he promoted the Ghost Dance, the agents thought, they would have a full-scale war on their hands. In December, Ghost Dancers at the Pine Ridge and Rosebud agencies asked Sitting Bull to join them. Fearing the great chief would spread unrest, an agent ordered the Indian Police—Indians recruited by the government to keep order at the agencies—to arrest him. On December 15, thirty-three policemen showed up at the chief's cabin. "I'm not going!" he insisted. When there was an attempt to rescue him, the shooting started. Sitting Bull and his teenage son, Crow Foot, fell dead.

With the death of Sitting Bull the Ghost Dance–inspired uprising slowed. But one more tragedy lay ahead for the Sioux.

The Seventh Cavalry's mission was to arrest Big Foot, chief of the Miniconjou Sioux band. Big Foot had been a Ghost Dance leader, but had given the religion up. He and 350 Miniconjou—most of them women and children—

One of the army's Hotchkiss guns and its crew after Wounded Knee.

wanted only to join Red Cloud at the Pine Ridge Agency. On December 28, 1890, the Seventh met Big Foot and his band near a creek called Wounded Knee.

For a tense night, the Indians camped, surrounded by five hundred cavalrymen. The Seventh's commander, Colonel James Forsyth, set up Hotchkiss guns—early model machine guns—on the hills. There was no possibility of escape.

As a bitterly cold morning dawned, Forsyth ordered the Indians to give up their weapons. The braves piled up some old, worn-out rifles. Forsyth wasn't satisfied. He thought the Indians had hidden their real weapons.

As the troopers began searching, a Sioux medicine man rushed forward. "Fight!" he shouted to the braves. "You

are wearing your ghost shirts! They cannot hurt you!"

Or so one report said. There are many different accounts of what touched off the massacre at Wounded Knee. According to one source, the soldiers found a brand-new Winchester rifle on a brave named Black Coyote, who waved it menacingly instead of giving it up. Others say a nervous cavalryman fired the first shot.

After that first shot, Wounded Knee exploded. The deadly Hotchkiss guns poured shells into the Indians as they tried to flee. A few may have escaped, but most—men, women, and children alike—lay dead. Between two hundred and three hundred Sioux bodies were thrown into a mass grave dug from the frozen earth.

Twenty-nine soldiers were also

killed, most of them victims of their own crossfire. Nevertheless, the army awarded seventeen Congressional Medals of Honor to the veterans of Wounded Knee. In a tragic way, the Seventh Cavalry had avenged the Battle of the Little Bighorn.

News of the terrible massacre soon reached Pine Ridge. Four thousand Sioux headed north to the border of the reservation, determined to make a stand. On December 30, they surrounded part of the Seventh. For a while it looked as if there would be a repeat of the Little Bighorn, this time in the wintry landscape of South Dakota. But the Ninth Infantry, a regiment of black "buffalo soldiers," marched all night and relieved the cavalrymen.

On January 31, 1891, General Nelson Miles and 3,500 soldiers arrived at Pine Ridge. The cold, dispirited Indians were disarmed and herded back to the agency. Miles ordered the Indians to watch as he paraded his men. As a bitter wind howled, the troopers and infantrymen filed past the Sioux. The show convinced the remaining Ghost Dancers that fighting would be futile. When the sun set below the bleak South Dakota horizon that day, the long fight had ended. The Sioux had been the last Indians to resist the tide of white settlement that had slowly swept across North America for centuries. The Indian wars of the Plains were over.

Wounded Knee Creek after the tragic massacre.

AFTERWORD

THE AMERICANS WHO REFUSED TO VANISH

The Battle of the Little Bighorn was a turning point not just for the Sioux, but for all Native Americans. General Custer's humiliating defeat forced the United States to look hard at its policy toward the Indians.

In the early years of the nineteenth century, the official policy was *removal*. The Indians of the Northeast and Southeast were removed, often by force, to the "worthless" lands west of the Mississippi River.

But soon whites began settling in the West. They demanded access to the "lands reserved for the Indians." The next policy was *concentration*. The Indians were forced onto smaller and smaller lands as the railroads advanced and towns sprang up. The Indians received compensation in the form of food and money. But this system, which was

Sioux Indians perform a flag ceremony at a South Dakota Pow Wow (meeting).

overseen by the Department of the Interior's Bureau of Indian Affairs, was often corrupt and inefficient. To many Indians, especially the Sioux and other Plains peoples, no compensation could make up for the loss of their land and buffalo.

In the late 1860s and early 1870s, some people began calling for a fairer Indian policy. Many western settlers, who lived in fear of Indian uprisings, scoffed at these reformers, calling them weak and unrealistic. They felt, as did General William Sherman, that "the only good Indian is a dead Indian."

Well-intentioned reformers did pressure the Bureau of Indian Affairs to replace dishonest and corrupt officials, sometimes with missionaries. Still, the Plains people continued to resist the government's efforts to take their land— resistance that climaxed at the Little Bighorn in 1876.

After the furor over the Little Bighorn died down, the reformers gained

Sioux at the Pine Ridge Agency around the turn of the twentieth century.

support. Critics pointed out that the conflict with the Sioux might not have taken place if the government had kept its word and obeyed its treaties. In 1881, Helen Hunt Jackson published a book called *A Century of Dishonor*, which was critical of the government's dealings with the Indians. Jackson believed that the Indians needed to become part of the mainstream of American society.

But how was this to be done? Many Indian groups, especially the Plains tribes, were hunters and gatherers; most white Americans were farmers or workers. Most Indians lived in close-knit groups that held property in common; white society prized free enterprise and personal property. A Mas-sachusetts senator, Henry Dawes, thought he had the answer.

The key to "Americanizing" the Indians, according to Dawes and his supporters, was to turn them into farmers. In 1887, Dawes sponsored a congressional act that divided reservation lands into individual "allotments" of land, held in trust for a number of years. Indians were encouraged to give up their traditional dress, customs, and religion and take up the whites' ways. To hasten the "Americanizing" process, Indian children were sometimes taken by force to boarding schools far from their homes. A new term, *allotment*, summed up this policy.

The Dawes Act was a failure. Some

Native Americans did take up farming. A few even prospered. But most resented the loss of their traditional way of life. In addition, greedy whites found loopholes in the law and swindled many Indians out of their land. The Sioux and other peoples became strangers in two worlds. The old way of life was gone forever, and yet few wanted to give up the culture that gave their lives meaning.

In the twentieth century, after World War II, a new policy, called *termination*, came into being. The government tried to terminate—that is, stop—payments and other benefits to Indians. They hoped the new policy would correct the abuses of the allotment system and make Native Americans more "independent." This policy, too, was mostly unsuccessful. Today, government policy toward Native Americans—a policy of self-determination without termination—is still a source of controversy and protest.

At the turn of the twentieth century the Sioux were barely surviving on their shrinking South Dakota reservations. Their birth rate dropped. Infant mortality, disease, and alcoholism—problems that still plague many Indian groups today—took a terrible toll. One anthropologist called the Plains Indians "vanishing Americans."

But despite continued and serious problems, these Americans refused to vanish. In the 1960s and 1970s, there was a renewed interest in the problems of the Native Americans. Public health measures improved birth rates as the general population dramatically increased. Indians began to reclaim their identity. Traditional religion and language made a comeback.

The Sioux were in the forefront of this new "Red Power" movement. In the 1960s, a young Sioux, Russell Means, helped found AIM, the American Indian Movement. The organization

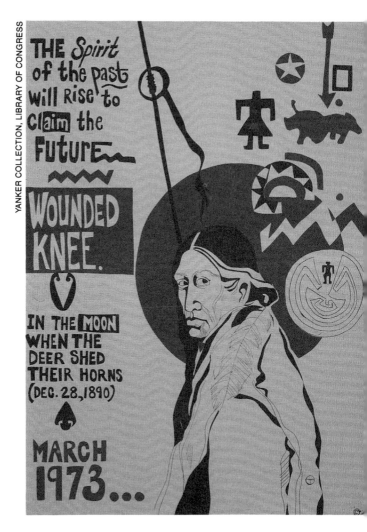

A poster commemorating the 1973 Incident at Wounded Knee.

Modern-day Sioux perform a traditional dance.

of Wounded Knee, on the Pine Ridge Reservation in South Dakota. On February 27, 1973, about 250 Indians occupied the village. Many of the occupiers were Oglala Sioux, descendants of Crazy Horse's band. For 71 tense days, the Indians crouched behind defenses, rifles in hand. Once again, whites and Indians fought each other. Once again, blood was shed: Two Indians died and one federal marshal was severely wounded before the siege ended. Many whites and Indians alike were angered by AIM's methods and the bloodshed at Wounded Knee. In fact, Russell Means lost in his bid for leadership of the Sioux's tribal council.

The Sioux have waged another battle, this one in the courts. The Sioux hadn't forgotten about the loss of the Black Hills. In 1980, after years of legal battles, the Supreme Court awarded eight Sioux tribes $122 million in compensation for the loss of their sacred land. But some Sioux still say that they will be satisfied only when the hills are given back.

The Black Hills have played a great role in the Sioux's history. They have been a sacred place for countless centuries. Sitting Bull and his warriors clashed with Custer at the Little Bighorn in their defense. Today, more than a century after that battle, the People of Dreams still look toward the *Paha Sapa* for inspiration. For, in the words of an ancient Indian song, "only the earth endures."

used radical tactics to bring attention to Indian problems. In 1969, Indian activists occupied Alcatraz Island in San Francisco Bay for 19 months. In 1972, AIM members marched on Washington along a route they called the Trail of Broken Treaties.

But the most dramatic incident happened at a place that already symbolized the Indians' struggle—the village

INDEX

Page numbers in *italics* indicate illustrations

SUGGESTED READING

Alvin Josephy's History of the Native Americans. Englewood Cliffs, New Jersey: Silver Burdett Press, 1989. (Six volumes, including biographies of Geronimo and Sitting Bull.)

The American Heritage Junior Library. *Indians of the Plains.* New York: Troll Associates, 1960.

Brown, Dee. *Bury My Heart at Wounded Knee.* New York: Holt, Rinehart, and Winston, 1970.

Connell, Evan. *Son of the Morning Star.* New York: Harper & Row, 1984.

Marrin, Albert. *War Clouds in the West.* New York: Atheneum, 1984.